Will Grace
& Jack Karen

Will & Grace
& Jack & Karen

**LIFE – ACCORDING TO TV'S
AWESOME FOURSOME**

Emma Lewis

Illustrations by Chantel de Sousa

Smith
Street
Books

Will Grace & Jack Karen

In 1998, when *Friends* and *Frasier* ruled sitcom land, *Will & Grace* arrived in our living rooms and changed the television landscape as we know it. Although the show centred on the friendship between lawyer Will Truman and designer Grace Adler, audiences adored the antics of Grace's socialite assistant Karen Walker and Will's out-and-proud best friend Jack McFarland. Jack and Karen soon became as central to the show as Will and Grace, and with incredible performances by guest stars like Debbie Reynolds and Molly Shannon, *Will & Grace* soon became one of NBC's highest-rating sitcoms.

There is no doubt that *Will & Grace* helped pave the way for future gay characters and storylines on prime-time TV. Before *Will & Grace*, there were no central gay characters on sitcoms. Even in TV-drama land it was rare to see gay characters in the early noughties, and rarer still to see two gay characters kiss. Remember the hype in 2000 when Jack and Tobey kissed on *Dawson's Creek*? The same year, *Will & Grace* showed the first gay kiss in a sitcom when Will kissed Jack for the benefit of news cameras during a protest. (Ironically, the protest was about a gay kiss being cut from a sitcom that Will and Jack were fans of.)

Great writing and stand-out comedic performances rightfully earned *Will & Grace* its place in pop-cultural history, but its impact is further reaching than that. Former US Vice President Joe Biden credits *Will & Grace* with educating the American public about LGBTI issues, and the Smithsonian has even included artefacts from *Will & Grace* as part of their collection detailing the history of LGBTI people in the United States.

After numerous accolades, including 16 Emmy Awards, the original series finished airing in 2006, but the popularity of *Will & Grace* in syndication proved that viewers weren't ready to say goodbye. The long-awaited return of *Will & Grace* in 2017 brought Will, Grace, Jack and Karen back into our lives, and audiences couldn't be happier.

So sit back, relax and enjoy some (at times, questionable) life advice and inspiration from Will, Grace, Jack and Karen, TV's awesome foursome!

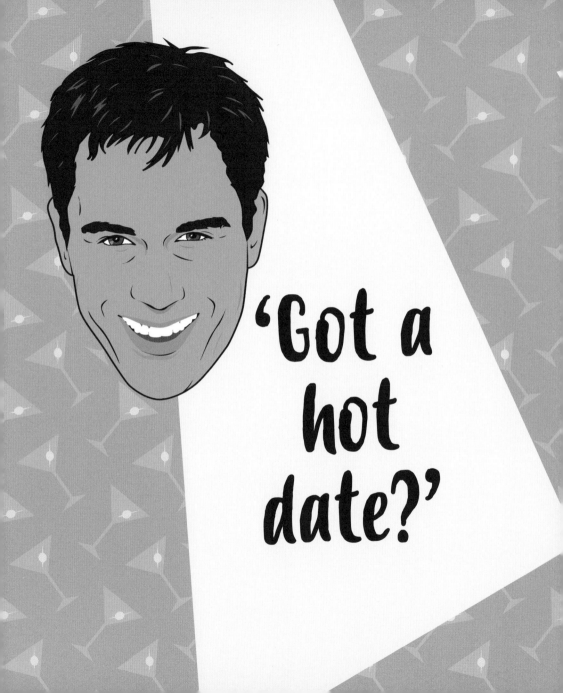

'No, but the guy who's dating me does.'

In the Beginning ...

Picture this: Columbia University, 1985. *Back to the Future* has just been released; 'We Built this City' is topping the charts; and *Miami Vice* is the coolest thing on TV. Will and Grace are at a college dorm party and have been dating each other for three months. Although Grace is a sophisticated woman who has had sex at least three and a half times, Will is reluctant to take their relationship to the next level.

Enter Jack McFarland. After discovering Jack literally inside his closet, Will and he get to talking. Jack tries to convince Will that Will is gay, but Will is adamant he isn't. Jack lays it out straight (so to speak): 'This well-worn copy of the *Dreamgirls* soundtrack begs to differ.'

Grace invites Will to Thanksgiving with her family, seeing this as her big opportunity to go all the way with Will. When Grace's mother Bobbi refuses to let Grace and Will sleep in the same bed, Will is relieved, but Grace is furious and ends up sneaking into bed with Will anyway.

Panicked, Will slips off to the bathroom and calls Jack for advice. Despite reaching out to Jack, Will still claims he isn't gay, but Jack knows Will is gayer than the day is long. Still in denial, Will goes back into the bedroom and throws Grace on the bed. Grace takes the lead (remember, three and a half times!) but it is totally awkward. Will says he thinks they should wait because he loves her. This only seems to spur Grace on – then Will suggests they wait until they get married. Somehow seeing this as a way out of sleeping with Grace, Will ends up proposing.

Downstairs, Grace tells her family the big news. Bobbi is singing show tunes; the neighbours are drinking champagne; and Will is filled with regret. Getting Grace alone, he finally admits he is gay. Grace is devastated and throws him out.

Cut to a year later. Will and Grace have not spoken since Thanksgiving. They run into each other at the grocery store near campus and, although their exchange is initially awkward, they realise they miss each other and their friendship is reborn.

Guide to Living with Your Best Friend

So, you've been besties since your age matched your shoe size, and you've decided to take the plunge and move in together. What could be more fun than sharing a home with your bestest buddy? Read on for Will and Grace's hot tips on making platonic co-habitation work.

Will says...

Making sure you still have your own space is crucial. It is SO important to maintain boundaries.

Grace says...

Within a week of moving into Will's apartment I demolished a wall and took over his bathroom.

Will says...

Even when things get tense, keeping the lines of conversation open is key. Just try not to make everything about yourself when pouring your heart out.

Grace says...

Are you talking about ME? It sounds like you're talking about me.

Grace says...

Try not to meddle in each other's love lives. All that matters is what YOU think of your new man!

Will says...

Easy to say for someone whose last boyfriend looked like he should've been guarding the bridge from the Three Billy Goats Gruff.

Will says...

Sharing food might sound like a great idea, and it probably is if you both have the same schedule. Try not to get into a situation where YOU do all the shopping while your roommate does all the eating.

Grace says...

Did you just go to Balducci's? I need some chicken.

Will says...

Know where to draw the line in terms of intimacy. It's okay to be close, but keep your roommate out of truly personal matters. Establish the boundaries early and you shouldn't have any problems later.

Grace says...

Can you come and have a look at this thing on my back? Bring tweezers.

Grace says...

Do you only have one TV? Sharing the remote requires extreme diplomacy. This can be a touchy subject, so proceed with care.

Will says...

Turn it back to *American Idol* or die!

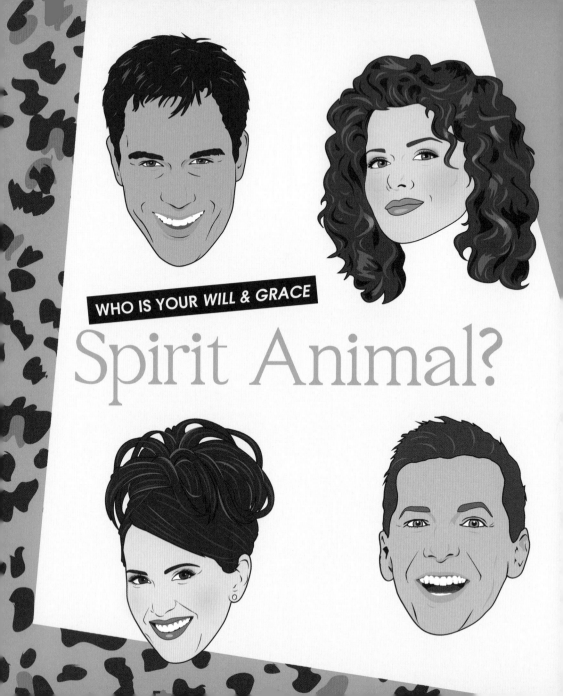

WHO IS YOUR *WILL & GRACE*

Spirit Animal?

Do you ever wonder if you really know yourself? Sure, you've been to paradise... but have you ever been to YOU? It's time to reveal your inner Will, Jack, Karen or Grace by taking this simple quiz.

1. **A close friend cancels plans with you at the last minute and you are stuck sitting alone at a fancy restaurant on a Friday night. What do you do?**

a. This is so my life. Vow to never speak to them again, then accept their grovelling apology an hour later and make plans with them for Saturday.
b. Who cares? Find the hottest waiter and get to work.
c. This is why I prefer to eat at home, at work, in the back of cabs and in bathroom stalls.
d. That doesn't happen to me, honey. Oh wait – it DID happen once, with some of Stanley's friends from the Hamptons. They mysteriously went missing around about the same time, actually. Nobody stands up the Walkers.

2. **Your idea of the perfect man is:**

a. Tall, handsome, funny, stable.
b. Hot, hotter, pays my cable.
c. Who am I kidding? Basically any guy who wasn't chosen by my mother.
d. Rich, connected and soon to be dead.

3. **What do you prefer for breakfast?**

a. Yolk-free omelette and a protein shake, preferably eaten alone.
b. I generally prefer something from Café Jacques, but whatever Will is making is usually the easiest option for a busy guy like me.
c. Whatever Will is making. I feel bad for him eating breakfast alone. So sad.
d. Vodka smoothie, hold the smoothie.

4. Your ultimate workout track is:

a. 'Somebody to Love' by Queen.

b. For butt-robics, definitely NSYNC, but for spinning class I prefer Frankie Goes to Hollywood.

c. I instinctively break into a run at the sound of Fox News.

d. Honey I don't work out. I was born this way.

5. Someone you barely know asks you to help them move apartments. What do you do?

a. This is my dream. I can have everything organised perfectly in their new apartment by 10 am tomorrow. Now let's talk curtains!

b. I once dated a guy who drove a moving van. He showed me inside a few nice apartments and I showed him inside my gym shorts.

c. How tall is he and what does he look like?

d. What side of 5th Avenue are they moving to? I'll have my driver block a few car spaces out front for the next 48 hours.

6. My bank balance could be best described as:

a. I've had a good year at work, but it could always be better.

b. Irrelevant, but let's say it's directly related to answer A.

c. Perfectly fine as long as Karen doesn't start cashing her pay cheques again.

d. Just like the universe – vast and ever-expanding.

7. My perfect night at home includes:

a. A fabulous dinner, a good bottle of wine and seven hours of *Designing Women* on TV.

b. Whose home? Cher's?

c. *Designing Women* marathon and a bucket of ice cream.

d. A liquid dinner and a new prescription.

8. **What's the worst job you've ever had?**

a. Representing someone who slipped on an upturned bucket of snow-crab legs at Red Lobster.

b. Human footstool at Elton John's birthday party.

c. Furnishing Barron Trump's nursery room.

d. Honey, I don't work.

9. **An old friend arrives in town unexpectedly, but you have an exclusive event that night that you can't bring them to. What do you do?**

a. Be a good person and begrudgingly spend the evening with your friend, but feel put out all night about missing the event.

b. Take them somewhere busy like Times Square and lose them in the crowd.

c. Palm them off to Will and hit the town.

d. Leave them at Park Avenue with Stanley, and catch up with them seventeen vodka tonics later.

10. **What's the most extravagant thing you have ever bought for yourself?**

a. Emporio Armani gym shorts.

b. A water bottle discarded by Madonna on stage during her Blond Ambition tour.

c. A canary-yellow asymmetrical dress I bought on impulse and haven't worn once.

d. A lovely antique chair I picked up somewhere. And by somewhere I mean Geneva, and by chair I mean ski lodge.

You are Will

You are smart, cautious and mostly very sensible. You have a lot of love to give, but sometimes your fear of getting hurt holds you back. You once apologised to a rack of winter coats after bumping into them at a department store.

'If I was going to have sex with a woman, it would be Hilary Swank... or Tobey Maguire.'

You are Jack

You are not afraid to be yourself in any situation – what you see is what you get. You are loud, outrageous and love being the centre of attention. Your denim cut-offs are cutting off your circulation as you read this.

You are Grace

You are unlucky in love, but that doesn't stop you from trying. You have a tendency to make situations all about you, but your friends adore you anyway. You have had spinach in your teeth since 11 am.

'I'm handing out lollipops and ass-whoopins, and right now, I'm all out of lollipops.'

'Honey, tact is for people who aren't witty enough to be sarcastic.'

You are Karen

You're a sassy little pocket rocket and you're not afraid to flaunt it. You have no vocal filter, and you're the life of the party right up until the point of passing out. You always have perfect hair and your lucky colour is greenback.

'I think the real mistake was when your father spotted your mother across a crowded swamp, dragged her back to his hut, and made you.'

Guide to Grooming

What are you looking at, sideburns? Never seen someone with money and soap? Sure, I make it look easy – but a lot of work goes into looking this good. I know, because I pay someone to do most of the work for me. Follow my guide below and you might just find yourself looking in the mirror at something truly spectacular.

Grooming budget. If you have to ask, you can't afford it.

Fashion. I've always said that husbands come and go, but the Chanel slingback is forever. Forget shopping anywhere that isn't on Madison Avenue, lest you die instantly in an uncontrolled friction fire from those nasty synthetic fibres.

Surgery. Don't be shy about going under the knife. Aging gracefully is for underachievers! If you're on the wrong side of 40 you're going to need a facelift and a neck lift. Can't afford the surgeon and need a quick fix? Keep away from chenille and backlighting at all times.

Hair. Be born with perfect hair like me. I'm sorry, I cannot help you any further with this matter.

Sleep. Look at those eye bags. I recommend doing something about that. Firstly, try some sleep. I like to get at least eight hours a night, between that last sip of vodka and that first time I'm shaken awake by Rosario in the morning. Failing sleep, see 'Surgery' opposite.

Makeup. Don't mess around with any of that drugstore garbage or you're likely to break out worse than 2007 Britney Spears at a Dairy Queen. How much should you spend on a good mascara? Whatever it takes to stop you looking like an extra on the set of *The Hobbit*.

Sun care. Stay out of the sun, unless you want to age a decade in half the time. There is nothing more unattractive than sunburnt skin and bad tan lines. No one wants to be seen with somebody who looks like they've been involved in the manual shutdown of a nuclear reactor.

Jewellery. My advice in two words? GO LARGE. Forget what J.Lo says – I'm all about the rocks that I got. I hear they have synthetic diamonds these days, but in my opinion, a precious stone doesn't pass muster unless it was hand-picked by orphans on the Ivory Coast.

Debra Messing

Debra Messing was born on 15 August, 1968 in Brooklyn, New York. She spent her teenage years acting and singing, with leading roles in *Annie* and *Grease* during high school. With her immense talent and strong commitment to academia, Messing graduated with a degree in theatre arts from Brandeis University, followed by a Master of Fine Arts at New York University.

Messing took up several minor TV roles after leaving college, and in 1995 was cast in her first movie, *A Walk in the Clouds*, alongside Keanu Reeves. Messing's big TV break also came in 1995, when she scored the leading role of Stacey in *Ned and Stacey*. Although *Ned and Stacey* only lasted two seasons, her role was well received and led to landing the part of Grace Adler in *Will & Grace*.

For her role as Grace Adler, Messing went on to win an Emmy in 2003 for Outstanding Lead Actress in a Comedy Series. After the original series of *Will & Grace*, she enjoyed several major TV and movie roles, and made her Broadway debut in the play *Outside Mullingar*. Messing has one child and is an outspoken political activist.

Did you know? Like many great comedy actors, Messing has starred in *Seinfeld*. She played Jerry's love interest Beth in two episodes.

'Rule number one.
Unless you're served
in a frosted glass,
never come within
four feet of
my lips.'

SMITTY'S
Cocktail
Menu

Smitty has served his fair share of drinks to New York's elite over the years. A rock and confidante to Karen, Smitty makes the best martinis in Manhattan and has a few other tricks up his sleeve. Want to pour all the classics with confidence? Follow his foolproof cocktail recipes.

SMITTY'S DRY MARTINI

ice cubes

60 ml (2 fl oz) gin

7.5 ml (¼ fl oz) extra-dry vermouth

7.5 ml (¼ fl oz) olive juice

2 best quality green olives

Chill a martini glass on ice.

Combine the gin, vermouth and olive juice in a cocktail shaker and stir.

Use a Hawthorne strainer to pour the cocktail into your chilled martini glass.

Garnish with two olives skewered on the end of a toothpick.

SMITTY'S OLD FASHIONED

1 sugar cube

1 dash of bitters

60 ml (2 fl oz) best-quality bourbon or rye whiskey

1 very large ice cube

1 slice of orange peel

Muddle the sugar cube and bitters in a short glass.

Add the whiskey and stir.

Place the ice cube in the glass and stir until the sugar is fully dissolved.

Garnish with the orange peel.

SMITTY'S MANHATTAN WITH A TWIST

ice cubes

60 ml (2 fl oz) best-quality bourbon or rye whiskey

30 ml (1 fl oz) sweet vermouth

2 dashes of bitters

1 maraschino cherry

Chill a short glass on ice.

Fill a cocktail shaker with ice. Add the whiskey, vermouth and bitters and stir.

Strain into your chilled glass and garnish with the cherry.

'I've got drinks piling up on my desk and a stack of pills I haven't even opened yet!'

Eric McCormack

Eric McCormack was born 18 April, 1963 in Toronto, Canada. He grew up performing on stage, and attended Ryerson University before leaving early to pursue a role with the Stratford Shakespeare Festival, where he remained for the next five years.

McCormack worked extensively on stage and TV in Canada before moving to LA in 1991. In 1994 he had a leading role in the hit miniseries *Lonesome Dove*, which spanned 43 episodes. It was on this set that McCormack met his future wife Janet Leigh Holden; they have a son called Finnigan, born in 2002.

McCormack continued to work in TV and movies in the United States before getting his big break in *Will & Grace* in 1998. McCormack has stated that he instantly related to the character of Will, and found many similarities between the two of them – pretty much everything apart from actually being gay! In 2001 McCormack won an Emmy for Outstanding Lead Actor in a Comedy Series.

After *Will & Grace* ended in 2006, McCormack returned to the stage and started his own production company, Big Cattle Productions. His leading TV roles include *Perception*, in which he starred as Dr Daniel Pierce, a research neuroscientist who solves crimes, and *Travelers*, a science-fiction drama where he plays time-traveller Grant MacLaren.

Did you know? Eric McCormack was a serious contender for the role of Ross on *Friends*.

Guide to Surviving the Holidays Single

Holidays can be a very stressful time for us all, particularly when single. The bickering, the constant questioning, the open discussion about your biological clock as Aunt Edna passes the potato salad – it can sometimes be too much to deal with in a single day. Avoid the drama and interrogation, and at least minimise the weeping with this handy holiday guide.

GIFTS

Grace: Manage expectations by delivering the bad news that you can only stay for two hours because you're squeezing three family visits into a single day to free yourself up for Black Friday shopping the day after Thanksgiving. The key is to announce your intentions to leave early, and before Aunt Abigail can guilt you into staying, present her with an enormous baked item that must be refrigerated immediately. While she's finding space in the fridge, quickly escape to another room.

FOOD

Will: While we're talking time management, let's look at the eating schedule. If you are making multiple stops during the course of the day, try to moderate your food intake at each event so you don't offend the following host by being too full. I remember when Grace helped herself to too many creamed asparagus tips at our first stop last Christmas and we had to make multiple stops on the interstate while she barfed at two consecutive highway Taco Bells.

ALCOHOL

Grace: It's probably best to avoid alcohol at the holidays. Unfortunately you won't be joined in your vow of sobriety by other family members, but it sure helps to be sober when navigating the awkward gaze of creepy Uncle Morty after one too many Brandy Alexanders.

CONVERSATION

Will: My golden rule is to keep the topics light and always try to change the subject before hearing a blow-by-blow retelling of your uncle's latest prostate complications. But heed my warning – even the most innocent conversation almost always leads directly to those dreaded words ... 'So, are you seeing anyone special?'

Grace: If avoiding the topic of romance fails, create a fictional new partner just to shut everyone up. My go-to this holiday season is a Jewish paediatric dentist who volunteers at homeless shelters. As a bonus, he gets along just great with Will's fictional boyfriend Raoul.

GETTING OUT OF THERE

Grace: Keep an emergency list of excuses for cutting visits short. These can be sudden illnesses with few obvious symptoms, or remembering leaving the oven on at home. Failing a good excuse, wait until everyone is distracted, find the closest unlocked window and make a run for it. A word of warning on the emergency exit; plan carefully, as I once destroyed a perfectly good purse after pitching it into a fishpond before vaulting out of a guest-room window.

Sean Hayes

Sean Hayes was born on 26 June, 1960 in Chicago, Illinois. He studied piano performance at Illinois State University, but left college early to become a music director at a local theatre. Hayes is an alumnus of Chicago improv troupe Second City and composed original music for the Steppenwolf production of *Antigone*.

In 1995 Hayes moved to Los Angeles, performing stand-up and taking various small acting roles. In 1998 he received acclaim for his role in the indie film *Billy's Hollywood Screen Kiss*, and was cast as Jack in *Will & Grace* the same year. Audiences were immediately drawn to Jack McFarland's outrageous antics, and like Megan Mullally, Hayes was nominated for an Emmy for Outstanding Supporting Actor in a Comedy Series for seven consecutive years, winning the award in 2000.

Since the original run of *Will & Grace*, Hayes has been busy performing on TV and in movies. He has also tread the boards on and off Broadway, and hosted the Tony Awards in 2010. Hayes married his long-term partner Scott Icenogle in 2014.

Did you know? When Hayes was first sent the *Will & Grace* pilot script, he tossed it in the trash because he was at the Sundance Film Festival and didn't want to fly all the way back to Los Angeles for the audition. Thankfully he auditioned eventually and scored the role. Phew!

GRACE'S

Guide to Running a Successful Business

Is your business floundering? Are you managing an assistant who thinks that a Long Island Iced Tea is an acceptable breakfast beverage? Look no further than Grace's guide to winning at business.

CREATE A BEAUTIFUL SPACE TO WORK IN

A cluttered, disorganised workspace really distracts you from your work. Sure, so does a gold-digging socialite who spends the day painting her nails and ignoring the phone – but what can you do? A clean and well-organised workspace is known to increase productivity. I also like to crack a window mid-afternoon to let the fresh air in (and Karen's vodka vapours out).

PLAN YOUR DAY

Being organised is so important. Since Karen is about as useful as a potted ficus wearing a Gucci brooch, I manage my own diary. I try to get my most challenging and unpleasant tasks (like chasing overdue invoices) done as early as possible, and save the tasks I prefer (like chasing the ruggedly handsome delivery guy) to do for later in the day.

STAFF MANAGEMENT

Speaking of Karen, a good chunk of my day goes towards managing my staff. From my trussed-up trophy wife of an assistant right down to the delivery guy I dated for three weeks who somehow neglected to mention that he had a wife,

it is important to treat everyone fairly. For Karen I try to be firm but fair, and for the delivery guy? Well, let's just say he won't be capable of lifting anything heavy for a while.

COMPLAINT MANAGEMENT

These days, if a troublesome client is still not happy, inevitably they will write you a bad review online. I was devastated the first time I got a negative Google review – how was I supposed to know the $700 table runners they changed their minds about three times were non-refundable? The best way to deal with complaints is to be the better person by not retaliating. Simply accept the criticism gracefully, binge-eat an entire cheesecake at your desk while sobbing, and move on.

NETWORK TO GROW YOUR BUSINESS

No matter where you go, don't be afraid to hustle. Even if you're attending your second cousin's *bris*, there's always an opportunity to get some new business if you notice the faded curtains and worn-out carpets. Where to draw the line, you ask? Maybe don't point out the tacky upholstery at an open casket.

A Day in the Life...

Ever wondered what time Grace misses spin class every morning, or what time Rosario tucks Karen into bed every night? If you fancy a sneaky peek into the everyday lives of the fabulous four, keep reading to find out what Will, Grace, Karen and Jack get up to on an average day.

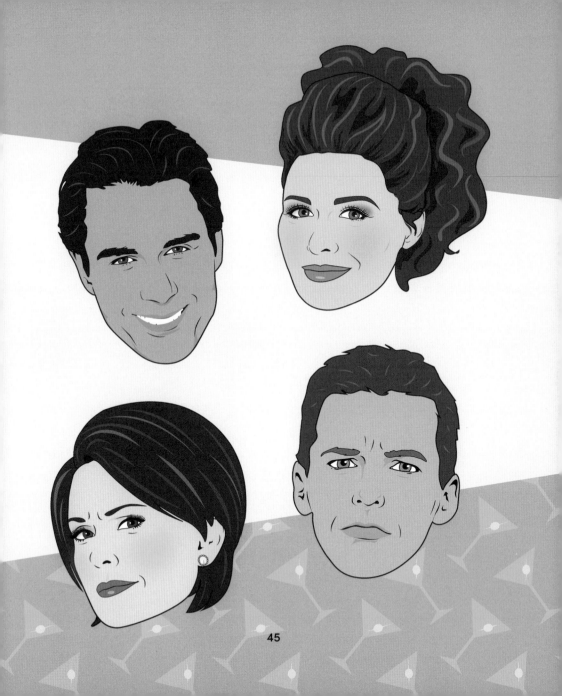

6.30 am
Grace's alarm goes off.

6.31 am
Damn it! Turn off Grace's alarm.

7.15 am
Make breakfast for one.

7.30 am
Serve breakfast for three.

8.30 am
Arrive at work.

11.45 am
Jack arrives looking for lunch, so I turn him away – I'm busy!

12.00 pm
Spend 30 minutes daydreaming about Charlie from Accounts.

5.30 pm
Pick up some groceries on the way home from work. Grace has spin class so I finally have some time to myself.

6.00 pm
Cook dinner for Grace, who is currently asleep on the couch.

8.00 pm
Hour-long moisturising routine begins.

9.00 pm
Grace is watching TV. I pity her sometimes. I should keep her company.

10.45 pm
Is that an ear hair? I don't think so. Spend 15 minutes in front of the mirror checking, just to be sure.

11.00 pm
Bed – one place I can guarantee to always get time to myself. Sigh.

6.00 am
Alarm goes off for spin class.

7.20 am
Wake up. Oops! Missed spin class.

7.30 am
Let's see what Will made for breakfast!

8.30 am
Arrive at work. Where is Karen?

11.40 am
Call Karen three times. No response.

12.00 pm
Sad desk lunch – can't afford to leave if Karen isn't here.

3.00 pm
Karen arrives. Wait – where is she going?

5.00 pm
I could catch the 5.30 pm spin class if I hurry.

6.00 pm
Arrive home. Oh, that's right – spin class. Skip it and crash on the couch.

7.00 pm
I should keep Will company for dinner, poor guy.

8.00 pm
I should get an early night, and get started on my book.

8.30 pm
Designing Women marathon on cable!

10.00 pm
Wake up to the sound of Will crying when Julia Sugarbaker tears apart Miss Georgia.

11.00 pm
Fall asleep after reading three paragraphs.

MY DAY ON A PAGE

Karen

7.00 am
Rosario pulls the curtains open.

7.05 am
Rosario screams in my face to get up.

7.06 am
Rosario draws a long bath and a stiff drink.

8.30 am
Driver takes me to hair appointment.

9.30 am
Return home, remember I have a job and head back out to the limo.

10.00 am
Coffee with Jack.

11.40 am
Ringing sound in ears eventually identified as Grace screaming at me on my messages. Head to Barney's.

11.30 am
Jack calls for lunch. Oh, why not? Call to cancel plans with Melania Trump.

2.00 pm
Time to stock up on office supplies! Stop on Madison to pick up diamond letter opener I can't stop thinking about.

3.00 pm
Work day begins! Walk in to find Grace in a mood. Not worth sticking around so head to Smitty's.

6.00 pm
Wake up face-down on the bar in a pool of Maker's Mark.

7.00 pm
Dinner with Rudy Giuliani.

9.20 pm
Wake up face-down on the bar in a pool of Maker's Mark. Smitty calls my driver.

10.45 pm
Valium and a dry martini while I slip into my silk nightgown.

10.47 pm
Slip down the stairs.

11.00 pm
Rosario carries me up two flights of stairs to bed.

7.00 am
Wake to the sound of last night's date slipping out the door.

7.30 am
Better keep Will company for breakfast. I pity him.

9.00 am
Disco Yogalates.

10.00 am
Coffee date with Karen, then I need to get some writing done. Open laptop.

10.05 am
Is that Ryan Phillippe? Come on, Jack – concentrate.

10.25 am
Search internet for defining image of early 1990s Kevin Costner, circa *Bodyguard*.

11.30 am
So bored. Call Karen for lunch.

12.00 pm
Lunch and a little shopping on Madison with Karen. Sulk until papa gets some new shoes.

5.00 pm
My work day is done!

6.00 pm
Bikram Jazzercise.

10.00 pm
Attend a one-man show starring a friend from improv class. It is so important to support other artists.

11.00 pm
Sneak out during the third tearful 'why didn't daddy love me' monologue. After another busy day, this gal needs her beauty rest.

'That's it — I'm done with men! I'm into women now. C'mon, let's make hot, hetero love to each other. Take off your breasts and turn around.'

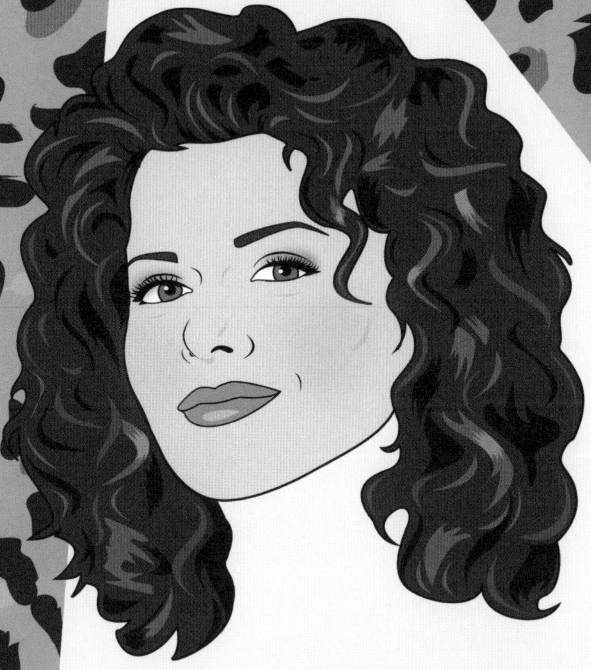

‘Oh, if only that was the first time a guy had said that to me.’

JACK'S
Guide to Jackting

Do you want to make it big on Broadway? Are you dreaming of fame, but need to take your acting skills to the next level? Here are a few pointers from a man who has performed to literally tens of people: Jack McFarland.

'It's not the Will & Grace show. It's called JUST JACK!'

METHOD JACKTING

Memorising lines is one thing, but in order to fully transform, you need to walk a mile in your character's shoes. Many famous actors do this, like the time Kevin Bacon spent three months disguised as a brooding high-school student in a conservative town. Just like Kevin, when preparing I like to fully immerse myself in the role. When writing my latest play, *Desperately Seeking Jack*, I chose to live exactly as a young woman in bohemian 1980s New York. This may have resulted in a restraining order from Madonna and being permanently banned from Battery Park, but a true *artiste* always gives his work everything.

IMPROVISATIONAL JACKTING

Being well practised in improvisation will give you the edge at auditions. I did try joining an improv group in my neighbourhood, but let's just say they had a few issues with some of the finer points of Jackting. How was I to know it wouldn't go over well when I wove some of my Ernie and Bert fan fiction into class one day? Get with the times, people – they were gayer than Christmas.

COSTUME AND MAKEUP

Sometimes on stage, less is more. There's no point wearing a full face of stage makeup if you're performing to three exhausted waiters on their dinner break and the stage is only two metres from where they're sitting. That said, how you present yourself is very important, so no expense should be spared when purchasing your outfit. At this point I usually cry until Karen takes me shopping.

LIGHTS. CAMERA. JACKTION!

It is important to check yourself before you walk out on stage. Last-minute nerves are normal, but too much stress means you could wind up looking more nervous than Donald Trump approaching the entrance of a wind tunnel. I address my nerves by splashing cold water on my face and giving myself a reassuring high-five in the mirror backstage. Just make sure the mirror is adequately attached to the wall, or your nerves could be further jangled by standing under a shower of broken glass (trust me, I speak from experience ... and I'm still picking shards out of my beret).

Megan Mullally

Megan Mullally was born 12 November, 1958 in Los Angeles, California. She studied ballet as a young girl, later attending college at Northwestern University where she studied English literature and art history. Throughout and after her time at college, she was active in the Chicago theatre scene.

After moving to LA in 1985, Mullally appeared in commercials before landing guest-starring roles on TV series such as *Seinfeld* (she played George's date Betsy when George was called out for 'double-dipping' his chip at a party), *Just Shoot Me!* and *Mad About You.* Mullally treasures her role on five episodes of *Murder, She Wrote*, which came when she was struggling to pay rent.

Mullally's big break came with *Will & Grace*, where her character Karen Walker became a TV sensation. Mullally won Emmys in 2000 and 2006 for Outstanding Supporting Actress in a Comedy Series – and was nominated for this award seven years straight! In 2000 Mullally met her second husband Nick Offerman while they were performing in the play *The Berlin Circle.* He went on to guest-star in an episode of *Will & Grace* while they were dating.

After *Will & Grace*, Mullally has been busy with many film and TV roles, and has put her unique voice to work in several animated features. Musically talented, Mullally performs regularly with her band Supreme Music Program, and with Stephanie Hunt in the duo Nancy and Beth.

Did you know? Mullally read for the role of Elaine on *Seinfeld* and was one of the preferred options before the part went to Julia Louis-Dreyfus.

Guide to the Devastating Insult

Are you ready to learn from two experts in the field of snappy slights? Let socialite frenemies Beverley Leslie and Karen Walker guide you through their step-by-step guide to the devastating insult.

HIT 'EM WHERE IT HURTS

Karen: Find their Achilles heel and focus your energy there. For example, a dear little teacup poodle like Beverley is particularly sensitive about his height, or lack thereof. Go straight for the jugular with their deepest insecurity.

Beverley: Equally, a washed-up, has-been hussy like Karen doesn't like to be reminded that the only reason she even made it in this town is all thanks to money that someone else earned, and toxins that someone else injected into her forehead.

INSPIRE ENVY

Beverley: I like to rile Karen up by subtly mentioning how my hefty new diamond ring keeps throwing me off balance.

Karen: Oh, yeah. You wouldn't want to slip and fall into something unfamiliar and cavernous. Like your wife.

THE BACKHANDED COMPLIMENT

Karen: Kill them with kindness before you knock 'em dead. For example. I just LOVE that jacket on you, Lucky Charms. Do they come in men's sizes?

Beverley: Thanks, Karen. And whatever your surgeon just pumped out of your upper arms looks great on your ass.

HAVING THE LAST WORD

Beverley: I'd love to keep chatting, Karen, but those of us who can see our reflections in the mirror need to go out and enjoy the sunshine.

Karen: You're just sad because the American Kennel Club hasn't recognised you as a breed yet.

Guide to Entertaining

Are you an expert entertainer, or are your parties a bigger flop than *Sharknado 7*? Let dinner-party master and host extraordinaire Will Truman take the pain out of party preparation as he guides you through his best tips for entertaining at home.

GUEST LIST

It's nice to have a mix of people whose personalities complement each other, so beware of clashes. For example, I like to entertain my work friends separately to my other friends, and try to avoid seating Trump voters next to actual members of the human race.

DRINKS

I always find that if I keep the drinks coming early in the evening, the conversation should flow nicely, and any awkwardness your guests might be feeling all but disappears. But if I keep too many drinks coming, Grace might end up telling everyone about her recent pelvic ultrasound, so I tend to restrict the stronger cocktails to before dinner only.

FOOD

Cooking up a storm is the best part for me. I like to go all out, spending the whole day preparing something really decadent. I do avoid cooking anything too rich, lest there be a repeat of the spicy lamb korma guest bathroom incident of 2006. The perpetrator is still unknown and currently at large in my friendship group.

AMBIENCE

Once your apartment is clean and dinner is in the oven, keep the music classy – I like a little French jazz – and relatively low in volume, so your guests can still converse. For a little extra ambience I might restrict access from Jack by changing the locks.

GAMES

Everyone loves a parlour game, right? Wait – come back! Okay, so maybe party games aren't for everyone. Learn how to read the room on this. If your guests start staring lovingly at the nearest door as soon as a game is suggested, back away from the Boggle immediately.

GETTING RID OF EVERYONE AT THE END OF THE NIGHT

Ply Grace with some of the booze you've been hiding from her and encourage her to offer up her extra-long rendition of 'Papa Can You Hear Me'. Evening over.

Celebrity Guest Stars

Will & Grace has always attracted an enviable list of guest stars from the stage and screen – so many, in fact, that they can't all be mentioned in a single sitting. So here are the top five.

1. DEBBIE REYNOLDS

Of course the number-one spot goes to Debbie Reynolds. She first appeared in season one as Grace's mother, Bobbi Adler, and such was her popularity that she returned for nine more episodes throughout the original series. You can read more about Debbie Reynolds on page 67.

2. SANDRA BERNHARD

The queen of the one-woman show, Sandra Bernhard appears as herself when her Manhattan apartment is up for sale and Will and Grace attempt to befriend her by making a bid they don't intend to follow through on.

When Bernhard finds out their ploy, she tears them apart in a hilarious scene where the saltier parts of her insults are bleeped out by the sound of a blender.

3. HARRY CONNICK, JR.

Go on, admit it ... we were all a bit in love with Leo, Grace's major love interest in the original series. Ticking all the important boxes for Grace and her mother alike (Jewish – tick; doctor – tick), Leo seemed almost too good to be true. Turns out, he was! Have any of us forgiven Leo for his infidelity when working for Doctors Without Borders? I think not.

4. KEVIN BACON

Jack, who has been stalking Kevin Bacon for some time (though he prefers the term 'professional crazed fan' to 'stalker'), winds up being interviewed to be the personal assistant of – you guessed it – Kevin Bacon. His encyclopaedic knowledge of the star sees Jack getting the job, and naturally, Jack's first task is to help Kevin find out who has been stalking him. Jack's job is short-lived once Kevin finds out who has really been hiding in the bushes. The episode culminates in Will and Kevin recreating the famous dance scene from *Footloose*.

5. CHER

As Jack is sitting alone in a cafe conversing with his Cher doll, the real-life Cher approaches him from behind. Not recognising her, Jack mistakes Cher for a drag queen, complimenting her on her flawless look. When Cher walks off unimpressed, Jack claims that he can do a better Cher than her. Jack's impression of how Cher should actually sound is one of the funniest *Will & Grace* moments of all time.

The Fabulous Debbie Reynolds!

Of the many notable guest stars who have appeared on *Will & Grace*, Debbie Reynolds stands out as one of the show's most memorable recurring characters. A multi-talented actor, singer and dancer with a career spanning over six decades, Reynolds was perfectly cast in the role of Bobbi Adler, Grace's over-the-top, show tune–singing mother.

Complete with a fur stole and towering bouffant, and seemingly always with Julius the accompanist by her side, Bobbi Adler became an audience favourite after her first appearance. Who could forget Bobbi's 'told you so' dance, applied with laser precision every time Grace doesn't take her mother's advice?

Writers made the most of Reynolds' dancing and singing talents, her comedic timing and her scene-stealing energy. Reynolds was so popular she starred in 12 episodes throughout the original series and was nominated for an Emmy for Outstanding Guest Actress in a Comedy Series Emmy in 2000.

Reynolds' death in 2017 – tragically just one day after her daughter Carrie Fisher died – brought an end to her long and illustrious career. In the 2017 return of *Will & Grace*, the show paid tribute to Reynolds with a few subtle nods, including a portrait of Bobbi Adler hanging in Grace's apartment.

Bobbi Adler, we love you and we're sure going to miss you.

Guide to First Dates After 40

We could all do with some good advice when it comes to navigating the treacherous terrain of dating – particularly those of us whose dating histories pre-date Swatch watches. Throw away your self-help book, it's time for first-date REAL TALK with Will and Jack.

GETTING A DATE IN THE FIRST PLACE

Will: Don't let Jack convince you that hook-up apps will lead to anything but heartbreak. Tinder is for the young and carefree – you're better off trying to meet someone the old-fashioned way, like making eyes at someone in the gym until they say hello (or in Jack's case, until they take out a restraining order).

Jack: Please excuse Will. He says things like that because he is fat and in love with me. What 'Failure to Paunch' over here failed to mention is that he's often jealous of the dates I score online. There's nothing wrong with a little internet fling, particularly when faced with dinner for one and pinot gris for three every Friday night for the last three years like someone I know.

LOCATION

Will: Picking somewhere classy sets the tone for who you are and what you want. Try a dirty martini at an upmarket hotel bar followed by dinner at an exclusive restaurant.

Jack: I hear the Dirty Shirley does two-for-one pineapple daiquiris on a Friday.

WHAT TO WEAR

Will: You don't want to give the wrong impression, so wear something stylish but low-key. Leave the leather pants at home; they allude to something you might not be trying to say.

Jack: Jeans so tight Freddie Mercury would blush if he made eye contact with you on the subway.

CONVERSATION

Will: We all talk about ourselves too much, particularly when we're nervous. Remember to ask questions and actively listen by using body language like eye contact and nodding.

Jack: No one likes a silent type. Go over the minutiae of your day, then spend 30 minutes reprising the highlights from your top-five dream Broadway roles.

THE BEDROOM

Will: Keep your cool! Sure, it might have been a while ... maybe.

Paris Hilton was still in diapers the last time you got lucky. Remember that being too keen (or too eager to please) can be a turn-off.

Jack: Impress him with your encyclopaedic knowledge of *Bull Durham*'s 23-minute sex scene.

REGRETS THE MORNING AFTER

Will: It would be rude not to say goodbye. Just be polite and try not to say anything that might commit you to seeing them again.

Jack: Check for concealed fire escapes and make a run for it before sunrise.

TO CALL OR NOT TO CALL?

Will: This is key – don't call too soon. You don't want him to think you're too eager – no one likes an eager beaver.

Jack: Send him seven Snapchats using the ever-flattering Bambi filter before you get home.

How Well
Do You Know
Will & Grace?

So you've watched your share of episodes and consider yourself a huge fan of TV's awesome foursome. But how much do you really know? Test yourself with our *Will & Grace* trivia challenge.

1. Who came out to their mother at an earlier age: Will or Jack?

2. Which famous TV actress does Karen refer to as her nemesis?

3. What was the name of Jack's follow up to *Just Jack*?

4. How many husbands did Karen have before Stan Walker?

5. What is the name of the only woman Will has slept with?

6. What is the name of the cafe that Jack runs out of his apartment?

7. What is Rob and Ellen's favourite restaurant?

8. What was Rosario's job on the night she met Karen for the first time?

9. What is the name of Bobbi Adler's piano accompanist?

10. Who is Will's favourite singer?

11. What was the name of the rare 'bashful geisha' figurine belonging to Will's mother that Grace accidentally destroyed when she set her drink on the mantel?

12. Which Monty Python star played Lyle Finster, Karen's love interest and father of Lorraine Finster?

13. Which character was once hired to star in an adult film in order to 'beat the old guy with a scrub brush'?

14. Jack's son Elliot was the result of a sperm donation. What item of clothing did Jack buy with the money he made from this transaction?

15. Who owns hair clippings from all four cast members of *The Golden Girls*?

16. What is Karen's maiden name?

17. Which items did Val Bassett ensure she got in her divorce because her ex-husband treasured them?

18. What is the name of Beverley Leslie's long-suffering wife?

19. Which band did Jack claim to be a member of the first time he met Will?

20. Which famous tennis star is Karen alleged to have dated in the 1980s?

WHAT KIND OF FAN ARE YOU?

0–5: *Will & Grace* **n00b**
Please quit your job and watch every episode immediately.

6–10: *Will & Grace* **enthusiast**
You've obviously seen a few episodes, but it's time to up your game. A *Will & Grace* binge session required – just think of what you're missing!

11–15: *Will & Grace* **super-fan**
Look, you've clearly seen every episode, but it's probably time to memorise them.

16–20: *Will & Grace* **expert**
Did you actually star in the show? You surely must have seen every episode multiple times. You, my friend, are a *Will & Grace* expert.

Who Is Val Bassett?

Val Bassett (played by the hilarious Molly Shannon), neighbour and occasional friend to Will and Grace, is a woman who is best summed up by her claim that she once lived in her storage space 'because of the millennium bug'. We first meet Val during season one, when Grace becomes snowed under at work and Will is feeling neglected. Will strikes up a conversation in the lift with Val, who has just moved into their building.

Will and Val become fast friends and Grace becomes more than a little jealous. Then comes the ultimate best-friend betrayal: Will partners with Val for a game of charades and they beat Will and Grace's former high score. At this point, things get a little *Single White Female*. Grace and Val fight for the coveted role of Will's best friend, which naturally culminates in a physical fight in which pointed insults are exchanged and outfits are ruined.

Molly Shannon appears as Val several times during the original series, with highlights including being knocked unconscious by Karen Walker after stealing a design from Grace; stealing Grace's music box (what can we say, she loves to steal things); and falling in love with Will's gay friend Jack after seeing his cabaret act, *Jack 2001*. Jack enjoys being the centre of attention, but things go too far when he awakens to find Val in his bedroom, wearing a vial of his bath water around her neck, and claiming that she was pregnant with his baby and had spent all day wearing his jockstrap as an oxygen mask (ewww!). Val returned in the 2017 season of *Will & Grace*, where Jack discovers that Val is now stalking somebody else: Karen Walker.

Fun fact: In *Seinfeld*, Molly Shannon played Elaine Benes' colleague who walked around with 'salami arms' in 'The Summer of George' episode.

Karen Walker
vs
Lorraine Finster

Nothing keeps a man happier than the somewhat conditional love of Karen Walker. On the other hand, nobody steals a husband like man-eater and woman-about-town Lorraine Finster. Both ladies have a thing or two to say about men, so heed their advice on how to find and keep your man, lest you lose out to the next gold-digging seductress who blows into town.

Karen: I've always said that if your genitals are on the outside, you're hiding something on the inside. Never trust what a man is saying, as it is unlikely to match what he is really thinking.

Lorraine: I disagree. I like to believe what my man says is true, particularly if it involves finally leaving his wife and meeting me on a yacht in Tahiti.

Karen: Listen, he is never going to leave his wife for you, so you should just give up now. It's not classy to steal another woman's husband – that kind of thing is for cheap hussies like Dame Judy Wench over here. The classy thing to do is keep an eye on the obituaries and find yourself a brand new next widower with a weak pulse and park views.

Lorraine: That's easy for you to say, you gold-digging, Upper East Side–dwelling duchess dowager. Unlike you, I like a bit of life left in my man, so I like to let 'em know exactly what they're missing out on if they pass me by. Always dress to thrill and you'll have them begging for more.

Karen: Like what, Lady Macbreath? Did you slide past seductively in your cheap cafeteria uniform when you seduced my Stanley in prison?

Lorraine: Maybe if what was beneath your frictionless Botox hide weren't older than the feudal system, you'd realise that men can see past your two-bit attempt at being sexy with those Prada heels designed for women a quarter of your age. Worse, you probably got them ON SALE.

Karen: How dare you, Saliva Doolittle! Where I come from, we don't just throw ourselves at the next trust-fund-baby-turned-geriatric-billionaire who trundles by on his motorised cart.

Lorraine: You did that yesterday!

Karen: You make a good point. Want to get a drink?

How to Survive a Breakup

Have you been dealt the crushing blow of betrayal by the love of your life? Have you just had your world turned upside down by unrequited love for someone you just can't get out of your head? Did you have a major crush on McDreamy and just can't get over the fact that he is NEVER COMING BACK? Well, pick yourself up off the floor and take a few pearls of post-breakup wisdom from Will, Grace, Jack and Karen.

Jack: Let's be honest – breakups are terrible. And just like Will's waistline, after you turn 30, it gets vaster and much uglier. At least there are a few things you can do in the short term to mend your broken heart. Firstly, you're going to need Will's credit card. After you've bought yourself a little something shiny, a spa day is in order. Karen normally pays for spa days but since I already have Will's credit card, maybe I'll treat Karen. Finally, it's time to pull yourself together, gussy yourself up and cut some hot shapes on the d-floor. As far as I'm aware, this is the fastest way to find a new man that doesn't involve phoning that guy from Craigslist who smells like basement and has two lazy eyes.

Will: I was so upset after my first major breakup that I stayed in bed for days. I cried so hard I could barely iron my jeans. It is SO important to avoid running into your ex at all during this phase – so staying in your bedroom is probably best. One day you will wake up and be ready to address those puffy eyes and get back out into the world. Hit the gym, buy a new wardrobe and then hit the gym again. The peak of this phase is when you want to ensure you run into your ex at all costs.

Karen: When Stanley and I got divorced, I was a wreck. You simply can't measure the feelings of loss I felt when it first happened – though my lawyers were able to translate it into a neat little dollar figure for me later. Still, there's only so much happiness that money can bring. Oh wait,

I just said that back to myself – how ridiculous! Of course the money will fix everything. You'll be fine, sweetie.

Grace: They say that some people eat their feelings, while others drink them. I have somehow mastered the art of doing both. At some stage you have to put down the chardonnay, pull yourself by the hair out of the cheesecake (sometimes Will does this part for me) and get back into dating. Just avoid anyone your mother chooses for you from singlejewishdoctors.com.

'There's no shame in getting old. There's only shame in getting ugly.'

Will

HAIR

Want Will's slightly preppy, flippy-floppy hair look? Keep it a little longer but neat, and use a lightweight product that builds a little volume on top.

WORKWEAR

A classic suit – tailored perfectly and costing more than a weekend in the Hamptons – should suffice.

CASUAL WEAR

A tight black tee paired with designer jeans defines Will's casual wardrobe.

EVENING WEAR

Will looks great in a slim-fit shirt. His evening look tends towards darker block colours, with navy and black suiting him best.

KEY ACCESSORY

Will can seriously carry off a leather jacket – remember the outfit he wore during the 'Midnight Train to Georgia' duet in Sandra Bernhard's apartment?

'Look at me.
I'm a freakin'
bombshell.'

Grace

HAIR

You're going to need big hair to perfect the Grace look – some natural volume and curls will certainly come in handy here. Tame frizz with a curl-enhancing product like mousse.

WORKWEAR

Grace's signature work look is a collared blouse with a short skirt and high boots.

CASUAL WEAR

Designer jeans and a tiny tee are staples for Grace's casual look.

EVENING WEAR

Pair a short skirt with high boots, or go for a dress that shows off those long legs!

KEY ACCESSORY

A long statement necklace looped several times around the neck.

'This colour really brings out my ass.'

Jack

HAIR

Jack keeps his hair relatively short and neat, with an area a little longer at the front for a touch of flair.

DAYWEAR

Did Jack McFarland single-handedly bring back the sweater vest? Pair a monotone vest with a patterned shirt and a pair of slacks that subtly allude to where all that work in the gym went.

WORKWEAR

When performing one of his trademark one-man cabarets, Jack keeps it simple and stylish by pairing a black turtleneck with black trousers. So chic!

EVENING WEAR

Pretty much the same as daywear, minus the sweater vest!

KEY ACCESSORY

Will's credit card.

'That's like saying Pradas are just shoes, or vodka is just a morning beverage!'

GET THE LOOK

Karen

HAIR

Karen has long, straight, shiny hair that looks great in an up-do. For extra volume, Karen gathers hair at the crown into a high pony.

WORKWEAR

You're going to need a killer designer skirt suit to pull off this look, preferably in a bold colour like pink or red. Don't forget very high heels with an even higher price tag.

CASUAL WEAR

Karen doesn't really do casual. However, a skirt paired with a sleeveless top to show off those toned upper arms should do the trick.

EVENING WEAR

Think eye-popping cleavage paired with a plunging neckline in a killer cocktail dress. Cropped jackets suit Karen's curvaceous figure perfectly. Don't forget gravity-defying heels to match that gravity-defying cleavage!

KEY ACCESSORY

A purse you could never afford, filled with cash you didn't earn.

AGONY AUNTS

Ask Jack & Karen

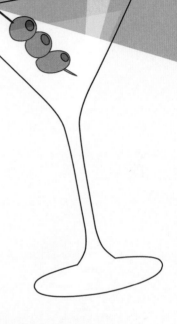

Do you have a burning question requiring the wisdom of an out-of-work actor and a partially drunk socialite? Pull up a chair at Café Jacques and get ready for a steaming hot cup of advice (with just a tiny splash of vodka) from your agony aunts Jack and Karen.

Dear Jack and Karen,
Help! I think I am in love with my colleague. I know it's a bad idea, but I can't help how I feel. What should I do?

Karen: Oh dear. I find this a little hard to answer because my only colleague is a seven-foot-tall maypole with questionable taste in fabrics, but hey, I'll give it a try. Although your feelings might be strong, work affairs at best will lead to a disappointing romp in the copy room, and at worst will lead to any associated copies being spread around the office like wildfire. Also, if you're sitting in the next cubicle to someone, you're probably both in the same pay-grade. Try to move up in the world, dear, not across.

Dear Jack and Karen,

I've just come out to my family, which went really well, but I wonder if I should also come out to my colleagues. I work for a large company that would be considered by many to be a little 'old school'. What should I do?

Jack: Congratulations on coming out to your family! You are living your truth and I'm proud of you. Coming out to colleagues can be hard, but it is definitely best done sooner rather than later as long as you are comfortable with them. You might be surprised to know that even I was a little shy about coming out to my colleagues back in '84. I went with something subtle – an interpretive dance complete with a *Flashdance*-style splashing-water effect. I can tell you now, my colleagues at Arby's could not have been more thrilled for me.

Dear Jack and Karen,

I've noticed since I started a busy new job that my drinking after work is slowly increasing. I rely on a bottle of wine to wind down, and I often turn up to work hungover. How can I cut down so that it doesn't start affecting my career?

Karen: Are you crazy? Why bother going to work if you can't reward yourself and unwind at the end of the day with a bottle of vodka? Oh, you said a bottle wine? Oh sweetheart, you amateur. Call me when you're so hungover you wake up face-down on a garbage barge heading out to Staten Island and then I might find some pity for you.

Dear Jack and Karen,

A close friend has recently gone through a big weight-loss transformation, and although I am happy for him, I cannot help but feel a little jealous. Am I the worst friend ever?

Jack: How revolting – is there anything worse than an overachieving friend exuding unbridled joy? Cut him off for a few weeks and get to work in secret. Cut out all carbs, avoid any non-essential hydration and hit the gym three times a day until you can fit into a pair of shorts so tight that the laws of physics no longer apply. Then invite him to have brunch somewhere that has flattering lighting.

A Tribute to Rosario Yolanda Salazar

ROSARIO:

'In my country,
I was a schoolteacher!'

KAREN:

'Oh yeah?
Well in this country,
you wash my bras.'

It is the year 1985. 'Some Like It Hot' by Robert Palmer and The Power Station is pumping on the dance floor. Karen is tearing it up with shoulder pads, enormous bangs and her killer moves. She has just fallen in love with Stan, and has to tell the Sultan of Boran that it's over. Once she delivers the news that she will no longer be Mrs Habibi Shoshani Padush Al-Kabir (or indeed, Mrs Martina Navratilova), Karen finds out that Stanley is married to someone else.

As Karen pours her heart out to the barman, Rosario, working as a cigarette seller, overhears her story and tells Karen in no uncertain terms that this guy will never leave his wife for her. The two get into a heated argument before Karen realises she may have met her match, and suggests Rosario come and work for her.

Rosario never left Karen's side after that moment, and the interactions between the two provided many of *Will & Grace*'s classic moments. Who could forget when Rosario was up for deportation, so Karen organised for Jack to marry her? As Karen herself so succinctly put it, 'You have to convince them that you two are a real married couple or this one's gonna be spooning ceviche out of a bucket on a dusty soccer field back in Chimi-Changaville.'

Shelley Morrison, who played Rosario, retired from acting in 2012 and did not return to the 2017 season of *Will & Grace*. In a heartfelt moment in the new series, we discover that Rosario has passed away from a heart attack. Karen is devastated, but hides her true feelings from her friends. If you did not ugly-cry during the tender moment when Karen finally says goodbye next to Rosario's coffin, you simply do not have a soul! Rest in peace, Rosario; we will miss you.

'I'm a little nervous. I'm breaking up with Ben tonight.'

'What's
the matter,
he's not gay?'

Smith Street Books

Published in 2018 by Smith Street Books
Melbourne | Australia
smithstreetbooks.com

ISBN: 978-1-925418-79-8

CIP data is available from the National Library of Australia.

Publisher: Paul McNally
Project editor: Hannah Koelmeyer
Editor: Katri Hilden
Author: Emma Lewis
Design: Giuseppe Santamaria
Illustration: Chantel de Sousa, The Illustration Room

Printed & bound in China by C&C Offset Printing Co., Ltd.

Book 66
10 9 8 7 6 5 4 3 2 1

Please note: This book is in no way affiliated with the creators or copyright holders of *Will & Grace*. We're just really big fans. Please don't sue us.